14 STONES

This is my story. This is my song.

BY CATHY J. HOLLABAUGH

ISBN: 9781790989324

ACKNOWLEDGEMENTS

Along with defining moments in life, there are always defining people in the midst of them.

To:

My Mom: Our time together was short but immeasurably important and irreplaceable. You gave me life and pointed me toward my Savior who would be the way, the truth, and the life for me. There is no greater gift you could have given me. Your smile and your laugh will always be a part of me.

My Dad: It was so easy to believe in a heavenly Father who would always be there, who loves me unconditionally, disciplines me out of love, and makes me feel special... because you did.

My Grandmother Brock: My example of faith, joy, and hope is the midst of unimaginable testing and trials. There was an unexplainable light and peace in your eyes that I could never understand. Now I do. Your prayers for me sustain me and manifest themselves in my life, even today.

To my children: A mother's love is as close as we come to understanding how much God loves us. A love so incredibly deep that He would give up His only son to die for the same people who crucified Him, and still do. I'm not sure I could do that. But I would die for you.

Lacy: My gift that just keeps on giving. You were my sweet, compliant, soft hearted girl who became my best friend. You made me feel like I must be the best, smartest, wisest mother in the world.

...And God laughed and said, "You should probably have one more."

Jay: My living proof that God truly does have a sense of humor. You have challenged me, questioned me, and entertained me from day one. God's greatest blessing usually come in a way we would have never imagined or expected. You are truly one of those. In a world with so few reasons to laugh, you have made me laugh until I cry and cry until I laugh.

Most importantly: Thank you to my Lord and Savior Jesus Christ who turned my mess into a message of hope.

CONTENTS

OH THE STORIES I COULD TELL...

Everybody has a story. A story full of moments, days, and seasons that become the definition of who we are, and who we will become, because of them. Defining moments.

We don't get to choose them. We just get to live them out. Some are heart breaking, gut wrenching, roads we would never choose to walk down again. But even those become our own beautiful story when placed in the hands of our Creator who teaches us that:

In all things God works for the good of those who love Him , who have been called according to His purpose". (Romans 8:28)

If we are teachable, every story has a lesson. And every lesson learned becomes wisdom.

When all the people had crossed the Jordan, the Lord said to Joshua..."tell them to take twelve stones from the very place where the priests are standing in the middle of the Jordan. Carry them out and pile them up at the place where you will camp tonight. (6) We will use these stones to build a memorial. In the future your children will ask you, "What do these stones mean? (22)...Then you can tell them, This is where the Israelites crossed the Jordan on dry ground .(23) For the Lord your God dried up the river right before your eyes, and kept it dry until you were all across, just as He did at the Red Sea when He dried it up until we had all crossed over. (24) He did this so all the nations of the earth might know that the Lord's hand is powerful, and so that you might fear the Lord your God forever". Joshua 4

In case I never get the chance to tell my children, grandchildren, or anyone who may wonder, I will lay these stones as a testament to what I have learned from the heart of God...so far.

FOURTEEN STONES

1

GOD'S VOICE

Don't let the noise of the world keep you from
hearing the voice of the Lord. *(John MacArthur)*

Song: You Gave Me Love *(Amy Grant)*

Do not be afraid for the Lord your God goes with you.
He will never leave or forsake you. *(Deuteronomy 31:6)*

I heard God's voice for the first time when I was twelve years old.

I always cringe a little when I hear someone say that God spoke to
them. Not that it is not possible. He certainly spoke in the Old Testament
to His people in an unmistakable way. Unlike those unquestionable
experiences, however, there was no burning bush and no loud audible voice
when He spoke to me. But, the effect was just as profound.

It began with a "Junior High" moment much like those that seem to
find every single pre-teen girl on the planet who is wading thru the
incriminating waters of middle school and pre-pubescent friends. It was my
first experience with hormonal insanity.

It changed me forever.

1

When I was in seventh grade, my parents divorced, and I had to attend a new school. The first year was good. I was given some honors, won a starting role on the basketball team, made cheerleader, and made some new friends. Life was good. Okay, let's just say life was okay, and the insanity was only mildly noticeable.

At the end of my eight grade year, however, the hormonally insane decided that sanity and peace on earth were just not an option. It began when a messenger for the boldly insane group informed me that I was wanted in the gym. I was led to a circle of girls who stood around me, and I quickly became aware that this would not be a fun game for me. It was more of a burning at the stake... with no trial. It was dodge ball with no place to run, and the weapon of choice would be words, words intended to steal, kill, and destroy. As I looked into the faces of the small town girls who had, up to this point, been my friends, they went down the line and each told me why they hated me.

Oddly enough, the only comment I really remember was from the girl who had been my best friend. It was something about my moving in and taking her spot as head cheerleader. She had decided to hate me over something of which I had no control.

It seems so trivial now, but the pain I felt was intense. She was the leader of the pack. Whatever rules she made was law for all the followers. I was a friendless outcast in one day. It was the 1971 version of mean girl bullying. Thank the good Lord it was before cell phones and the social media that becomes the cross upon which young people are crucified today.

I can also see the face of a friend that I had known and loved since kindergarten, with her head bowed and shame evident in the depths of her eyes. I knew she did not want to be a part of it, which she told me the next day, but standing up... and standing out... is often the hardest thing to do. At that age, we mostly just take comfort in the fact that today it is someone else who is under attack, and we are given the reprieve of just one more day.

So many times, bullying is about the uncontrollable; the child who can't help their looks, their family, a disability, or whatever makes them different. God forbid that we should be different. It can simply be jealousy. People don't need a reason to hate. It is often how people feel better about themselves. They only feel good when they make someone else feel bad. It is an age old story.

I had lost my family, lived alone with my Dad twenty-five miles from school, and now my "friends" had all turned against me. I felt abandoned by the world.

Abandonment would become the spider in the middle of my "cobweb of dysfunction" throughout my life.

I rode the bus home and went in to an empty house on a cold winter day. If I close my eyes, I can feel the cold concrete floor as I slid down beside my bed, put my head on my knees, and sobbed. It was the darkest, loneliest place I had ever been in my young life.

It was also my first experience of the light of Jesus shining brightest when it is the darkest.

As defining moments go, it is a day I will never forget. The devastating hurt of abandonment, loneliness, unworthiness, and hopelessness enveloped my young girl's heart. It was deafeningly silent and intensely cold.

But as I sat in the still, cold silence, I felt the weight of a hand on my shoulder. The hand was warm and comforting and strong.

In the depth of my broken heart and the quiet stillness of my hopeless thoughts, I heard God say:

"I will never leave you or forsake you. I will always be with you."

Stranger still, as I think back on that calming whisper, I am sure that I had never read that scripture. I would have never thought of the word "forsake." It is possible that I had heard it spoken in church, but I was instantly convinced that it was God speaking to me in his King James language. In fact, I had no doubt then, and I have no doubt now.

There were things about me that changed that day, and, in many ways, I was never the same. I never really trusted girls as friends from that point on. I changed schools and had a hard time trusting anyone as a friend. I still do.

More importantly, that was the day that I knew that the love of God was the one thing I would always be able to count on. I knew I would always be able to trust Him without the fear of abandonment and rejection. It was the beginning of the realization that God's love is not about me.

*"God does not love us because of our goodness, or kindness, or great faith. He loves us because of **His** goodness and kindness and great faith. You cannot do anything good enough to make God love you more or anything bad enough to make God love you less. Only HE has perfect, unconditional love."*
-     Max Lucado

Thirty seven years later, it is Christmas Eve 2009.

This is my first Christmas Eve without my family. My husband and I have separated after 33 years together. My grown children are snowed in at their grandparent's house due to a very unusual "white Christmas" in Texas.

I walk out onto the porch of my newly rented single-wide trailer, and the moon is reflecting, brilliantly, off of the snow. The stars are beautiful, and the night is so still and quiet. A silent night. This should, once again, be one of the darkest nights of my life. It is not. I am overwhelmed by the beauty and assurance of a loving God who sent His son to earth on this night that we celebrate as Christmas Eve, so long ago. The same God who once again touches my shoulder and whispers to my heart, "I am still here. I will never leave you or forsake you." I know exactly what "forsake" means.

I just smile, with a true peace in my heart, and whisper, "I know Lord... I remember."

Peace on earth was real in my heart.

2

Going Home

There is no place like home when the people who live
there make "building one another" their highest priority. *(Gordan McDonald)*

Song: House That Built Me *(Miranda Lambert)*

We are not happy here because we are not at home here.
We are not happy here because we are not supposed to be
happy here. We are like foreigners and strangers in this world. *(1 Peter 2:11)*

Not long ago, I made the statement, "I just wish I could go home, but I don't know where that would be."

The house that I grew up in is no longer there. It burned to the ground in the 1980's. The last time I was there was in 1975. There was never an opportunity to revisit the place of my greatest, and worst, childhood memories. In actuality, I never wanted to go back. The coldness and darkness of my last years there left me with nothing but a sincere need to escape and build a new home. A real home. A safe place that would be full of love and security and warmth.

And, if home is where the ones you love are, that was not possible either. My grandparents, mom, and dad left this earth many years ago. My children were grown and on their own, and no matter which way I looked, I could not see home.

I realize now that it is the *feeling* of home that I long for. All my life, I have longed for that feeling.

I never felt like I had the home that other people had. I had images of the two story house with the white picket fence, flowers in the garden, Mama in the kitchen when I came home from school, and the smell of homemade bread in the oven. There would be big family reunions and Christmases filled with decorations, lots of presents, and singing around the piano. Mama and Daddy would kiss under the mistletoe.

Oh I had moments of childhood that were priceless. I grew up in an old country rock house that my great grandparents built in the early 1900s. The floors were concrete and wood, and the air conditioning was the air that came through open windows in the hot Texas summers. Well, there was a lot of hot wind, but there was nothing to "condition" it! We had propane floor heaters which took an hour to heat a room, and they were turned off at night while we slept under electric blankets. My dad would come through and light the heaters in the morning before waking us up an hour later.

Summers in West Texas could be brutal. I remember standing in front of the mirror trying to put on makeup, and the sweat running down my face so fast that the makeup just rolled off as fast as I could slap it on. Many nights, my brother, sister, and I slept outside on cots down by the creek.

Most of my greatest memories of childhood centered around that creek. It was called "Dead Man's Creek." I'm not sure how it got that name, but that couldn't have been a pleasant story. It was not far from the house, and the water ran year round. There were a couple of times when the creek flooded to within a few feet of the back door.

But for 3 kids, alone for the summer, it was as good as Hurricane Harbor, Six Flags Over Texas, and Colorado river rafting rolled into one glorious form of entertainment.

Honestly, I can't even imagine leaving three young kids alone with rushing water, snakes, fish, turtles, and horses. It was a different time. We swam, fished, swam the horses, used the horses for diving boards for hours at a time, and camped out under the stars. We had no television (well only 2 channels that were black and white and fuzzy), no video games, and no McDonald's fast food. If we needed a snack, we rode the horses about three miles to the Hamby store. We caught horny toads and smashed large tarantulas with a baseball bat to watch their legs fly off. Who needed video games?!

When I think about it, we lived in a house next to a hill called "Rattlesnake Hill" next to a creek called "Dead Man's Creek," and my parents left us alone there all summer. Maybe they thought that if they needed to, they could just make more children!

Those are the memories I hold on to. But, the heat of those long Texas summers was never as unbearable as the emotional coldness inside that house. Apart from each other, my parents were good people. They were talented, beautiful, intelligent people. But, together there was a cold ugliness between them that was terrifying to me.

I'm sure there were some great family times. I do remember one week when we were snowed in and spent a week at home playing games, doing puzzles, and huddled around the fire. For a short time, we talked, laughed, and sang. I felt the teasing warmness of a real family.

The normalcy of that week stood out among the contrasting dysfunction of many other weeks. Most of my young girl memories were of hostility and ugliness. My parents did not speak to each other and lived totally separate lives. When they did speak, it often ended in screaming and violence.

Many years later than it should have happened, my parents divorced. I have a vivid memory of sitting in my dad's lap and my mother telling us to choose who we wanted to live with. I was speechless. I was so overcome and so devastated that I could not utter a word. In that silence, my mother looked at me and said, "Well I can see you have made your choice." And, she left. My sister was graduating from high school and married soon after.. My brother had two years of school to complete, but he opted to move in with a friend.

My home was no longer violent. It was silent… and cold… and empty. I remember an eleven year old girl standing in the dark, waiting on the school bus, her breath fogging the panes as she looked out the door. I see her coming home after three hours on that same bus to a cold house and lighting that old propane heater, praying she doesn't blow herself up, and shivering for the next hour until it is warm enough to remove her coat and gloves. In some ways, the memory of the cold and the emptiness of that house never left me. That is why, for so long, I saw her and felt sorry for her, but I did not own the feeling. It was just too hard.

Yet I still long for a chance to go home.

"When all of the earth turns against you… all of heaven turns toward you. To keep your balance in a crooked world, think of home."
- Max Lucado

What I realize now is that it is not the reality of the past that I long for. I do miss my parents and grandparents unbearably. But it is the "ideal" of home that I long for, as does every human being. It is a safe place where I know I am loved, without conditions, just as I am. It is a secure place where my father hugs me and says, "Don't worry. I will take care of everything, and it will all be okay." It is a place where I don't have to be in control and responsible for everything in my life, a place where I am surrounded by family and people I love.

I know now, within the depths of my soul, where my home is. That perfect home and perfect family we all long for. I long for it, and look toward it, knowing that I will never be satisfied until I walk through the gate. The pearly gate. My heavenly home.

I wouldn't be surprised if it has a creek, or river, running beside it. The river of beautiful, eternal, life.

God created us with an emptiness and a longing for home that will never be satisfied here on earth.

Shall we gather at the river?
No snakes this time.

3

What If God Says No

I asked God to take away my pride, and God said "No."
He said it was not for Him to take away but for me to give up.
I asked God to make my handicapped child whole, and God said "No."
He said her spirit was whole and her body was only temporary.
I asked God to grant me patience, and God said "No."
He said patience is a by-product of tribulation. It isn't granted, it is earned.
I asked God to give me happiness, and God said "No."
He said He gives blessings; happiness was up to me.
I asked God to spare me pain, and God said "No."
He said suffering draws you apart from worldly cares and brings you closer to me.
I asked God for all things that I might enjoy life.
He said He gave me life that I might enjoy all things.
I asked God to help me love others as much as He loves me.
And God said, "Ahh, now you have the idea."
(Author Unknown)

Song: Trust His Heart *(Cynthia Clawson)*

Trust in the Lord with all your heart and lean
Not on your own understanding. *(Proverbs 3:5)*

Defining moments of tragedy and devastation, in the world, always seem frozen in time.

I vividly remember where I was, what was happening, who I was with, and from whom I heard the news when:

- the Challenger exploded on national television with the first civilian passengers on board
- the buildings were blown up in Oklahoma City
- the terrorists attacked the World Trade Center on 9/11
- and the day that Shawn McMullen died.

Our world was affected and changed by the first three. My life and my definition of faith were changed by the last.

I have loved the Lord for as long as I can remember. But this was the moment that started my real journey to come to know myself, what I really believe, and the true nature of the God that I believe in and serve.

Shawn McMullen was a young cowboy who, to the world, looked destined to be a World Champion. Not only was he loaded with talent, but he was also one of the good guys. He was one of those rare young athletes who knew what he believed and wasn't afraid to let it be known or share it with others.

It's hard enough to try to make sense of why a young man, destined to make his mark on the world, would be allowed to die so young. But for me, it was so much more. His death was the birth of my doubt and fear. I was overwhelmed by the possibility that God will not always keep evil from happening to His children. How do you have the faith that can move mountains when God just might say "no?"

Shawn's mother Glenda was, and remains, a faith walkin', faith talkin', sold out woman of God. You know, the kind that a lot of people would call a "Jesus freak." Freak is a word that describes someone who doesn't conform or fit in a world that demands conformity.

She talked of "praying in the spirit" and "claiming" the truth and promises in the word of God. She talked of miracles and healing, and she shared her faith with anyone and everyone who would listen. She was a faith hero.

When I was a young woman trying to start a music ministry, she talked to me about my calling and my need to finish whatever I did with a call to salvation, or my efforts would be in vain. She talked to me about praying with expectation. She told me of miracles of healing that allowed Shawn to become the NIRA National Intercollegiate Rodeo Association's Calf Roping Champion after suffering a knee injury. I knew the strength of her faith. I knew she prayed for Shawn daily.

Then, on a late night drive that is a part of the life of a professional rodeo cowboy, a drunk driver instantly ended the earthly life of Shawn McMullen.

The woman who had the faith that could move mountains lost her only son.

I was not a part of the family, and I would not have been considered a close family friend. However, my heart was broken for the loss of a young life that held so much promise and for the heartbreak of a family that I could not even imagine.

This tragedy represented a loss that was devastating in my life.

I did not lose my son. I pray that God will not ask that of me.

I lost my unquestioning faith.

I did not lose my faith. I lost my *unquestioning* faith.

Everything changed in that moment. My safety zone with God no longer felt safe. If this could happen to a woman of such strong, unwavering faith, then my children, and nothing I held dear in this world, was safe.

Fear and anxiety overwhelmed me. It suddenly became reality to me that God could always say "no."

If you reach a place in your own life where you feel strong and secure in your faith, then Satan will try to move into other areas of your life where you are most vulnerable; those places where he can destroy you. He knows where we are weak. And almost every mother's weak spot is her children.

On that late night in 1996, the woman with the strongest faith I had ever seen... lost her only son. My doubt and fear was not that God didn't exist, or that He didn't hear, or that He didn't care. My distress was the knowledge that God does exist, He does hear, and He does care, but, for reasons we may never know or understand, God allowed this tragedy to happen. To Glenda's prayer of protection, God simply said "no."

So, I diligently began a search for answers. In one week, I read, *When God Doesn't Make Sense (James Dobson), Where is God When I Hurt (Philip Yancy),* and the story of Job in *The Holy Bible.*

I just couldn't accept that being a Christian did not guarantee all the right answers, perfect protection, and a life that was void of tragedy. What was I supposed to cling to?

I'm not sure where I got the idea that if you were a strong Christian, with a strong faith, you could claim and believe in a life void of tragedy. I was new to the name it, claim it faith that I had been hearing about. That is what I thought Glenda believed, I understood that she believed it was the strength of HER faith that decided how God answered her prayers.

I could have just read the word of God. Only the verses taken out of context come anywhere close to saying that.

Dr. James Dobson states in his book, *When God Doesn't Make Sense,* that he has seen few other circumstances in life that equal the agony of a shattered faith. It is a "crisis brewed in Hell." It leads directly to what he calls "the betrayal barrier." In his opinion, 100% of all believers will go through a time when they feel like God has abandoned them, or it seems that God has let them down. He went on to say that 90% of us never recover.

I thought that Glenda McMullen must surely feel betrayed by the God that she so loved and served.

We drove to Shawn's funeral with heavy hearts. People began to whisper about how Glenda had gathered some fellow believers together to pray for the resurrection of Shawn; the same way that Jesus had raised Lazarus from the dead. I can honestly remember thinking that God was giving all the scoffers plenty of reason to believe that Glenda's God didn't exist.

I just believed that He existed but had chosen to be absent. If not absent, then at least silent.

I also knew that Glenda and her family were in the midst of other devastating things in their lives, and that Glenda's husband Kenny was in the hospital for stress related issues when Shawn was killed. I was sure that this would be the end of a life of faith as they knew it.

When I went in to that funeral, I could hardly breathe. I thought this was going to be one of the worst days of my life. It's not that I had not lost loved ones, or been to funerals, or experienced hardships in life. I had experienced plenty.

I think I was afraid that my life would never be the same either. It wasn't.

I have never experienced a funeral like Shawn's funeral. The music, the testimony of his friends as to what a great influence he was on so many, and the tribute to Shawn's brief life was amazing. Yet, my heart was heavy with disappointment and disillusionment.

> Disillusionment: a feeling of disappointment resulting
> from the discovery that something is not as good as one
> believed it to be. (Webster's Dictionary)

As the anointed music and the spirit of God began to fall over the auditorium, Glenda and Kenny McMullen stood to their feet with hands raised to their Lord and King to signify their heart for the God they loved. They began to silently praise and worship the God who had said "no."

This in spite of the fact that He had taken their only son.

To this day, 15 years later, I cannot think of that scene without crying and wanting to fall to my knees. If I have ever heard anything audible from the spiritual world, I believe I heard it in that moment. I actually heard, in my ears, and in the depths of my very soul and spirit… the applause of Heaven.

I was overcome and overwhelmed by the shame in my own doubt. I sat in amazement at the display of faith, spoken silently but boldly, in that moment, by a mother who was asked to make the ultimate sacrifice. She will forever be in my heart as a faith hero. I KNOW that Glenda and Kenny McMullen will one day hear, "Well done, my good and faithful servants."

My life and my faith were changed forever by that moment. Glenda's message, much like the one Job received, was that sometimes in this life we may never know all the answers because we are not God. It has to be enough that we know the One who does have all the answers.

Most importantly, even when the answer is "no," God still loves us. He has a plan that is good. We are only asked to trust His heart. Trust the heart of a God who sacrificed His only son, willingly, for a people as unworthy as we are; a God who understands loss, and pain, and sacrifice. Trust the Creator of unconditional love.

I'm sure that those who witnessed Jesus' crucifixion on that Friday that He was crucified had no idea what would happen on Sunday. The greatest plan of redemption, salvation, and restoration appeared to be a very cruel, senseless tragedy to those that witnessed it. They did not know the perfect plan of God any more than we do.

And the end of that story changed the world.

I have learned that the times that seem the darkest are when we see God the clearest because He IS the light. In my eyes, Glenda's story was a little like Job's.

In the story of Job, God allowed him to lose everything he had, but in the midst of it all, He gave him the one thing that could never be taken away.

> If Job ever wonders why God doesn't bring back the children
> He had taken away, he doesn't ask. Maybe he doesn't ask because
> he knows that his children could never be happier that they are in
> the presence of this One (God) that Job had seen so briefly.
> Something tells me Job would do it all again if that's what it took
> to hear God's voice and stand in His presence.
> For God gave Job more than Job ever dreamed… God gave Job Himself.
> Faith is not trusting that God will always do what we want…
> It is trusting that God will do what is right.
> - *Max Lucado*

Shawn's death started my journey toward letting go of my belief that if I could just be good enough, and remain faithful, that God would keep all the bad stuff out of my life. I have come to know, with each storm, and each trial, that it has nothing to do with me or anything I can do. It is about how good God is. It is about how little we know and can understand.

I continue to try to draw closer to Him in the midst of every storm. He continues to show me His heart.

There have been times when I have stood in the midst of the most violent and devastating storms in my life and just raised my hands to heaven and said, "God I don't understand where you are or why this is happening to me, but I am going to praise you... for you are my only hope."

I will forever be grateful to Glenda McMullen for teaching me about that kind of faith... even when God says "no."

For the past 20 years, Glenda and Kenny McMullen have held a memorial roping in Shawn's honor. Glenda would tell you that many, many people have come to know the Lord, beginning with Shawn's funeral, and continuing with each and every church service that is held at those ropings.

Ironically, his death has probably saved more people than anyone will ever know.

There was a story told at Shawn's funeral. I'm not sure what night this happened. It might have been the night they left that last rodeo; the night he died.

Shawn's traveling partner was driving, and Shawn turned to him and said, "Do you know where you are going?"

The young man answered with the name of the next rodeo to which they were headed.

Shawn said, "No... I mean when you die?"

The young man said, "Yes, I do... Heaven."

Shawn replied, "Me too."

4

𝒜 Better 𝒜nswer

The only time my prayers are never answered
is on the golf course. *(Billy Graham)*

Song: Say Amen *(Brian Free and Assurance)*

But truly God has listened, He has attended to
the voice of my prayer. *(Psalm 66:19)*

Shortly after Shawn McMullen died, as I continued to seek understanding concerning doubt and fear, I experienced another defining moment in my life of faith journey.

At this point, my time, purpose, and my heart centered around my family. But I never seemed to be able to totally give up my love for training barrel horses.

Throughout my childhood, much of it spent alone in the country, horses had always been an important part of my life. They were my friends, my confidantes, my companions, and they always seemed to love me, much like a loyal dog, even when I messed up.

My opportunity to own good horses was limited by the amount of money it takes to go through enough colts to find that especially talented individual that it requires to be competitive and successful. The trainers that have many colts to choose from every year have much better odds of finding the superstar. I usually only had one. Sometimes it took me five years to have three colts in hopes of having one winner. People in the horse world know the kind... the ones that are born with the ability to easily do what you ask them to do with willing hearts, willing minds, and natural talent. These are the ones who make you look like a real trainer. These are the ones that teach you more about life, and what it takes to succeed, than you can learn from any manual or clinic. They don't come around very often.

So even though my life was busy and full with children that I adored, and the things involved in keeping a husband on the road living his dream, I had been blessed with three talented individuals (horses) who needed to be hauled. This is a necessary process we call "seasoning" that allows a horse to become accustomed to the different conditions that he will be asked to compete in.

As any mother and wife knows, it is challenging to make it all work when your time and commitments are pulling you in so many directions. There is always a mother's guilt involved with anything she chooses to do for herself. It was with all those conflicting emotions that I set out to take these colts to a three day event in Austin, Texas.

I started the trip by heading to the barn to load horses and finding my little roan mare with her head hung between the fence and the gate. She had been there for some time, and her head was the size of a watermelon. I loaded her and the others and drove to the veterinarian's office where I dropped her off. I was told she had a pretty serious head trauma and would have to be watched really close through the night.

From the time I woke up that morning, I had a sense of dread and foreboding and just felt like I shouldn't be going. This incident just added to that sense of uneasiness.

However, I had a lot of money in entry fees and two other nice horses, so I convinced myself it would be stupid not to go.

After I got to Austin and put the horses up, I needed to go to the convenience store. I had traveled a lot by myself and had never had any hesitation or fear of being alone in a big city.

But this day, I just couldn't shake the feeling that something bad was going to happen. I ran in and out of the store convinced that maybe a robbery was about to happen.

So I had been praying. All day, from the time I left home, I prayed for protection and peace. It didn't help matters that I also kept reminding myself that the last time I came to this barrel race I had fallen and broken my arm and shoulder. That memory did nothing to ease my anxiety and fear. Maybe this was an "unlucky" place for me.

Looking back, I believe there was some serious spiritual warfare going on around me.

The next day, I was getting ready to run the first horse, and I had saddled and tied him in a stall. When it came time to warm up, I went into the stall to put his protective boots on. I bent over and pulled the Velcro on the boot. The next thing I knew, I was crawling out of the stall with a bloody nose and a bashed in face.

I had now been to this barrel race twice and had yet to make a run. I have, however, visited the emergency rooms at both of the major hospitals. I'm just sayin'.

Two weeks later, after facial reconstructive surgery, I was in church for the first time since the accident, and the first song they sang was *God Will Take Care of You*. I got up and went outside to sit on the steps and wept.

Still reeling from Shawn's death, for the second time in a matter of months, I asked, "Really God? Will you really take care of me? Then where were you when I was praying for protection? Are you there? Do you really care about someone as insignificant as me?"

And, for the second time in my life, I felt the hand of God and the voice of God speaking to my heart. I plainly understood, "Cathy, (that's what God calls me)... I spared your life."

In the doctor's office the next week, my surgeon looked at me and said that there was no real reason why that blow didn't kill me, and it very well could have. I know there was a reason. I prayed fervently, and God was there. I believe in my heart there was a spiritual battle taking place over me ,around me, and for me, and that is why I was so troubled on my way to Austin.

We were never promised a life without pain and suffering. We were only promised help thru the battle, peace in the midst of fear, strength in our own weakness, and eternal victory in the end. Really, what more could we ask for?

If everyone who was a Christian was given a life free of trouble, would we love God only for what He could do for us? Wouldn't everyone want to be a Christian for that reason? Would that be real love?

We can never know all the ways of God. I don't think we were meant to.

That's where faith comes in. Faith grows from being tested. His ways are not my ways, but they are perfect.

I am reminded every day when I look in the mirror. A face that is a little more scarred and battered is a small price to pay for a heart a little closer to God and a soul a little closer to peace.

I can be free of fear because I know how my story will end. God can say no, and it can all be taken away. None of it was mine anyway. Whatever I have is a gift from God. Anything taken away on this earth will be restored immeasurably in heaven.

It will not be the last time God's answer is "no." Sometimes it may be "yes" or "wait," but there will always be an answer.

Grace. Mercy. Eternal life. The ultimate answers. The things that matter most. God saying, "I've got this, and I've got you."

The best answer of all.

5

The Best Teachers I Ever Had

Have thine own way Lord
Have thine own way
Thou art the potter, I am the clay
Mold me and make me after thy will
While I am waiting, yielded and still
(Old hymn by Adelaide Pollard)

Let the wise listen and add to their learning.
Let those with understanding receive guidance.
(Proverbs 1:5)

Horse Sense: What a horse has that keeps him from
betting on people. *(W.C. Fields)*

I once read a book called *All I Really Need to Know I Learned in Kindergarten* (by Robert Fulghum). Well, I can say everything I ever needed to know about life, relationships, trust, loyalty, and heart, I learned from a horse.

Even though I was born with a fairly competitive spirit, I never had the desire to be a world champion barrel racer. I never gave much thought to competing at the NFR even though I had a couple of horses that probably could have gotten there. My husband was the one born with the talent and those goals that he would give anything to achieve. My love has always been simply for the horse itself.

I had a desire to understand how a horse thinks. My joy was in taking a young horse and working with him every day to see what he would develop into. It must be the same desire that everyone who is called to be a teacher feels. So I fell in love with teaching.

After many years, most trainers learn that the great ones are born not made, and they end up teaching us more about barrel racing than we teach them. What I realize now, at the end of my training years, is that they taught me more about life than I could have ever imagined.

We are all born with certain abilities, talents, and strengths that help, or hinder, our search for our purpose in life. We all have a purpose. Discovering, developing, and achieving what we were created to do is the ultimate dream… and the ultimate dilemma. It is also at the heart of peace.

Each of us in an original. (Galatians 5:26)

God made you unique. Society says, "you can be anything
you want to be." But, can you? If God didn't pack you with
the meat sense of a butcher, the people skills of a salesperson,
or the world vision of an ambassador, can you be one? An
unhappy, dissatisfied one perhaps. But a fulfilled one? No.
Can an acorn become a rose? A whale fly like a bird? Or
lead become gold? Absolutely not. You cannot be anything
you want to be. But you can be everything God wants you to be.
(Max Lucado)

Just like us, every horse is unique. They are certainly not all created to be a barrel horse. But, I learned something from each and every one.

My first really great barrel horse was a colt my dad bought for my mom at a horse sale for $100. She called her Button because "she was cute as a button" (that's a mother for you). I never really knew her pedigree, but she had a brand from the Spade Ranch in West Texas, which indicated she was probably not bred for speed. But what she lacked in that department, she made up for with quick turns and consistency and, of course, heart.

"Heart" is the greatest trait of every great barrel horse.

Initially, that quickness, combined with a tendency to turn and run when scared, was the reason none of us wanted to ride her. However, she matured quickly, and when my other two horses had a heated physical disagreement which ended in crippling each other, I was forced to ride her.

She understood the concept of running barrels quickly, with very little help from me, and made the exact same run every time. She made me, at thirteen years old, look like a barrel horse trainer.

She took no wasted steps and had no silliness. She just got the job done in the most efficient way possible and gave it 100% every time. From her, I learned that sometimes it may not be enough, but it is so important to never have to look back and wonder if you could have tried harder. She was a happy, successful, little girl's dream of a horse. From her, I learned to love barrel racing and to love a horse with a winner's heart.

Ten years later, and several very average horses in between, my next teacher (and blessing) came in the form of a beautiful red roan mare named Sweet Kinda Bugs. I am a sucker for a pretty horse. And, at 2 years old, looks and breeding are about all you have to go on. She had both. She was bred to be a race horse and looked like a roping horse. She was also very quiet and very talented.

But there were a couple of things I learned quickly. She did not like people. Oddly enough, she was an orphan colt, raised on a bottle, but she did not want to be anybody's pet. She would not kick or bite or be belligerent in any way. She just made it clear that she wanted to be left alone.

If she were a person, she would have been my favorite cartoon character on the greeting cards, Maxine. She would have spoken her mind in complete bluntness and honesty with absolutely no need for approval from others. As long as she did her job, I was okay with that. And, she was outstanding at her job. I knew her heart, and I knew she loved me because she wanted to please me. She just wanted no public displays of affection.

I have a friend whose husband told her, "I told you I loved you when I married you, and, if I change my mind, I will let you know." I wouldn't have recommended that sentiment if you expect your marriage to last, but I have a feeling Miss Bugs would have been fine with that.

I distinctly remember making a practice run on her, as a 3 year old, when I was getting her ready for the futurities. It was so good, I got off and laid my hands on her, asked God to protect her, and to give me the wisdom and ability to stay out of her way. If I am being honest, it was one of those "Oh Lord, please don't let me screw her up" kind of prayers. And I thanked him for the gift.

The second lesson I learned from her was about kindness and patience. If she didn't understand what you were asking her to do, or you tried to use force excessively, she would just STOP and do *nothing*. I mean she wouldn't move. But if you showed her and gave her a chance to figure it out, she would die trying to please you. A man who wanted to just jerk and spur and force her into submission would have gotten nothing from her... absolutely nothing. Now there's a lesson for men trying to have a relationship with a beautiful woman!

She won over $100,000 running barrels and poles, ran until she was 14 years old, and was so crippled she could barely walk. I imagine if you brought her up out of the pasture at 21 years old and headed her into the arena, she would give it everything she had. She was the epitome of heart, perseverance, determination, and sacrifice. She was beautiful inside and out as long as everyone understood what she asked in return. "Treat me right, with love and respect, and I will love and serve you until the day I die. And don't pet me; I hate that!"

Looking back, it is amazing to me that the three greatest horses I owned come to me back to back. The next one was a little cutting bred mare named Quixotes Toya. She also was not bred for speed but could turn a barrel as fast as she could run. She was very intelligent. Within 30 days, she was running barrels, and I mean *running* barrels, and telling me how it should be done. There was only one problem. About one out of every three runs, we knocked a barrel over. She didn't anticipate or cut you off, which is a barrel racer's nightmare, she just turned so quick that she drug them over. She placed at several major futurities and would have won another had it not been for a hit barrel.

I tried everything: spurs, whip, different bits, different saddle, kicking harder, not kicking at all... everything I knew to try. The problem was, the harder you pushed, and the more she thought she was in trouble, the harder she turned. If you rode two-handed all the way into the turn, she would almost throw you over her head when she turned. I actually went off on one occasion. All barrel racers know what it means to get "dash-boarded."

So, one day, my husband was going to show me how to ride her all the way past a barrel. He had said several times, "Can you not just ride her one step further into the turn?"

Yes, he is a calf roper. You know the story. It was one of those discussions that ended with, "if you think it's so easy, why don't you just do it?"

He said "okay." (Insert smiley face emoji here.)

So he whipped to the first barrel, and it was beautiful (I was really dreading having to hear this story for the rest of my life). Feeling very proud and confident at this point, he whipped harder and further to the second barrel. As was her pattern, she turned so hard and fast (while he was still whipping) that he ended up in front of the saddle, on her neck, upside down, with his legs straight up in the air.

It was one of the greatest moments in a wife's life. I laughed so hard, I was crying. When he finally slid off, he handed me the reins and said (and I quote), "That bitch is harder to ride than she looks." Priceless.

In frustration, and a never ending need for money, I sold her to a young girl who never gave a thought to "not hitting a barrel." She just relaxed and had fun on a great horse. She let her do her job and showed me how useless worrying about what might happen can be.

When you focus on fear and what *could* happen, you create circumstances that make that very thing you fear a target. Then you crash right into it. It's like the baseball coach saying, "Just don't strike out." Suddenly, striking out becomes the focus of all his thoughts, and that fear is much more likely to manifest itself.

> You can't depend on your eyes when your imagination is
> out of focus. *(Mark Twain)*

Riding (and living) without fear, having simple faith and trust, and not worrying about what **could** happen allows good things (and good horses) to happen.

The third really good horse I had was a horse they called Preacher. He was a young horse I bought after he had already placed at the first futurity he was ever entered in. He obviously had tremendous talent. He had only been in training for about 7 months and was sort of a freak. You had to be very careful and patient in the way you handled him because it didn't take much for his wires to cross and for him to totally panic. But, when he was "on," there was no horse on earth that could get around a barrel like he could. I had a lot of fun running him, and luckily, the one thing I do have is patience. In Preacher's case, that was a virtue.

Reacting in anger to anything Preacher did was not going to end well. And, unlike Miss Bugs, Preacher would hurt you. I would not call him mean, he was just violently reactive. Realizing that his *fear* manifested itself in wild reactions allowed me to enjoy one of the most talented horses I ever rode. I tried to make sure he felt confident and secure and that he trusted me.

There were times when he outran everyone by a half second. There were also times when he ran up the fence and was disqualified. He was a little "off" somewhere in the recesses of his mind. But the times that he was "on" made it all worth it. Many of the greatest horses in history were very freaky and quirky, and he certainly proved that theory.

When I sold him, it took a couple of different riders to find one who understood him. He was making his mark in the pro rodeo world when a foot abscess caused him to have to be put down.

A life of promise cut short is heartbreaking in all the arenas of life.

As my daughter started to compete, my focus became keeping her on the horses that she needed. Fortunately, Miss Bugs filled that role well for many years. The thrill of watching the two of them, who I felt were both my children, win championships were some of the best moments of my life. I naively thought because I had several good colts in a row, that there would always be another great one, and I could easily find and train another winner.

Instead, I learned why the trainers that win year after year start with many, many colts to find one good one.

I also learned some life lessons from some of the common, untalented, and just plain bad ones.

Just like people, some horses just seem to be born with a mean, strong-willed nature. Others are simply not talented in the way that makes good barrel horses. I only had one that I considered pure evil. His name was Sonny.

According to his breeding and looks, Sonny should have been the perfect barrel horse. His pedigree contained the best breeding in the barrel horse world. He was that beautiful deep golden color with a flax (white) mane and tail. When I bought him at 3 years old, he was so intelligent that if you tapped him on the shoulder, he would shake hands (with his foot) like a dog.

But there was one fatal flaw in Sonny. He was evil. His beauty and perfection were so unimportant when matched with an evil, unwilling spirit and a cold heart. He had no desire to do anything other than what he wanted to do. And, he was sneaky and deceptive about it. He seemed like the most docile, sweet animal until he caught you off guard Then, when you least expected it, he would try to kill you. His intelligence was used in the most sinister way. No amount of training, brilliant teaching, or coaching was ever going to change Sonny's heart because Sonny, for whatever reason, had no heart.

Much like Satan, on of God's finest creations, he chose his own way. Beautiful, talented, and evil. I sold Sonny in a barrel horse sale and told everyone who asked me not to buy him. Sometimes people think the only thing a horse like Sonny needs is a good trainer. I hope they were right. But I have a feeling that Sonny has dealt a lot of people misery in this life, much like that beautiful, talented, fallen angel that seeks to destroy all of us.

There were several others after Sonny but just none that were noteworthy. They were not evil, just nothing with the talent. Honestly, I don't even remember some of them.

However, one of my very favorites is one that is still with us, completing his story, as I write this chapter. Noah is the second colt out of Miss Bugs. Noah is the opposite end of the spectrum from Sonny. Much like Sonny, Noah is the result of perfect planning for the perfect barrel horse. He is beautiful, and his breeding is the result of a cross between two amazing barrel horses in their own right. Unlike Sonny, however, Noah has the kindest, most willing heart.

They say that horses have two innate instincts that manifest themselves when they feel threatened. They are "fight" and "flight." When Noah was a few hours old, I walked up to where he was laying, and, when he saw me, he jumped up (not wobbly at all) and ran, as fast as a deer, away from me (and his mom). It was very unusual for a baby to run so far away from his mother and to be *so* frightened the minute he stepped into this world.

However, Noah has no fight response. He is a pleaser with a beautiful, willing, and kind spirit. He is the most talented athlete I ever sat on. He has it all: speed, athleticism, endurance, and he will go until you say stop, or he will die trying. He just has that one major flaw that was evident from the day he was born: fear.

He has unreasonable, unfounded, innate fear. When he sets his focus on something he is afraid of, he loses his ability to think rationally. A fear becomes irrational if you have been shown that it is unfounded and unnecessary, and you continue to live in a fearful state.

Noah very seldom relaxed or trusted anyone to show him what situations and things were safe. He has very little faith in his master to guide him. Often, his fear gets in the way of his talent and willing heart, and it controls him.

> I am the Lord your God, who hold your right hand and I
> tell you... don't be afraid... I will help you. *(Isaiah 41:13)*

> When I am afraid, I will trust in You. *(Psalm 56:3)*

We are very much like Noah sometimes... so full of fear of what could happen or might happen. When that fear consumes our thoughts, we may just come to the end of our time here and realize that we missed the beauty of the journey and the opportunity to succeed in the way God intended.

> The only thing we have to fear is fear itself. *(Franklin Roosevelt)*

Noah has more ability than 90% of the barrel horses I see today. But if he does not come to the point of calmness, peace, and trust, he will never fulfill his potential. All of his God given talent will be wasted.

I read once that 90% of the things we fear and worry about the most never happen. Even though God gave us the instinct of fear as a survival mechanism, when unfounded and unnecessary, fear rules our lives. It overrides all the other gifts and abilities we have been given. It becomes what controls and enslaves us.

Although Noah's story is "to be continued," I believe in my heart that, with enough time and patience and unconditional love from his trainers, Noah will blossom and become the champion he was born to be. The same amount of patience and unconditional love that our heavenly Father gives to us. I pray for wisdom for his training and that Noah can let go of his fear and fulfill his potential and possible destiny. But, just like us, in response to

the guiding and teaching of our master, the final choice will be up to Noah.
****

As is so often the case, some of my hardest and most profound lessons came when I handed the reins to my daughter. The "thrill of victory" and the "agony of defeat" played out in HER life became my greatest lessons of blessings and brokenness.

These defining moments in the life of this mother and daughter require a chapter of their own.

The last two champions who affected our lives, love, and faith in the most profound way were named Petro and Petey.

6

The God Who Gives and Takes Away

PETRO & PETEY

It is doubtful whether God can bless a man greatly
until He has hurt him deeply. *(A.W. Tozer)*

Song: Praise You In This Storm *(Casting Crowns)*

I consider that our present sufferings are not worth
comparing with the glory that will be revealed in us. *(Romans 8:18)*

Petro was a miracle... one of those rare gifts. He was born to run barrels. It was so easy and natural for him. How we came to own him was another one of those gifts straight from the hand of God.

Miss Bugs had been such a blessing to our family. Her winnings had allowed my kids to rodeo. Together, she and my daughter, Lacy, had accumulated quite a resume, and Lacy was given a full scholarship to rodeo for Tarleton State University. Unfortunately, after many years of traveling, Miss Bugs was just not able to do it anymore. She had run for 10 years, most of which had been battling very sore feet and legs, and we just couldn't ask her to keep going in that much pain. She didn't deserve that.

In order to keep her scholarship, Lacy needed another barrel horse.

To compete in the toughest college region in Texas, it had to be a good one. In reality, those kinds of horses cost more than any house I ever lived in. If we could have afforded that, we would have lived in a better house.

Strangely enough, after being involved in an accident that could have killed all of us, we were given an insurance settlement that allowed us to buy another horse. The amount was not huge, but it at least gave us the opportunity to buy another one.

So, praying for guidance and divine intervention, the search was on.

As I sat in the stands at a barrel race, I saw a horse run that really caught my eye. For many reasons, other than the obvious decent time he had run, he just had the look of unlimited potential. Latricia Duke, who just happens to be one of the greatest trainers of all time, was sitting beside me and I asked if she knew the horse. Just so happened... it was her sister-in-law.

William Paul Young, author of *The Shack,* would say, "Coincidence has a name."

She also told me that it was a horse with great potential, and there was a possibility that he would be for sale. The owner's name was Denise, and they called the horse Petro.

I walked out of the building and found Denise and Petro, explained to her my circumstances, my limited amount of money to spend, and how much I liked her horse. She hesitated, then with tears in her eyes, she said, "You know, I had hoped that I would never have to sell him, but because of some unforeseen circumstances, I just may have to. On the way here, I began to pray that if that is what I had to do that God would send me someone that Petro would be as much of a blessing to as he has been to me."

Sometimes God says "yes". This was the one.

After a little negotiation, and possibly some divine intervention, we had a deal.

At the first college rodeo, Lacy hit a barrel but would have finished in the top three. At the second one, she won the barrel race convincingly. I distinctly remember sitting in the stands, crying and thanking God for the unbelievable gift. Not only was he good... he was exactly the kind that all barrel racers spend their lives hoping, wishing, and looking for and very few ever find.

I never for one second took it for granted. I was simply grateful and humbled, and I promised to give God, each day, all the glory. Isn't that always what we do when we get exactly what we want?

I knew there was going to be glory.

Petro was a superstar.

What I later learned was that sometimes we glorify God through triumph and victory, and sometimes we are asked to glorify Him through brokenness and defeat. There are blessings in each. And, God works in mysterious ways.

I felt that God had blessed my child and, in doing so, blessed my mother's heart even more. I was daily brought to tears of gratitude and thanksgiving for the gift.

It was summertime, and the rodeo season was in full swing. Lacy and Petro were winning everywhere they went. One day a young man told me that Petro was going to be a name everyone in the barrel racing world would know someday, like Scamper and Bozo. I knew how rare and special he was.

> I've learned that we must hold everything loosely, because
> when I grip it tightly, it hurts when the Father pries my
> fingers loose and takes it from me.
> (*Corrie Ten Boom*)

In August, four months after Petro had come to us, Lacy told me she was leaving around 2:30 p.m. to go to a rodeo in Athens, Texas. I was working, and I remember looking at the clock around 2:30 and praying for safe travel and protection for Lacy and Petro and those that she traveled with.

Around 6:30, she called again. I will never forget the sound of her voice. Mothers just know.

She said, "Mom, Petro fell, and he's hurt bad." She was too upset to continue, so she put Latricia (yes, the same one who was there when I saw Petro for the first time) on the phone. She confirmed that it looked really bad, but they were going to put Lacy and Petro in their rig and meet us at the veterinary clinic in Weatherford, Texas.

Beautiful people and beautiful acts of kindness always seem to be around (strategically placed) in the midst of tragedy.

Everyone was right... it was bad.

After many x-rays and discussions about not wanting any animal to be saved only to live a life of pain, the decision was made to put Petro down.

As I looked into those beautiful, soft, eyes of a champion and watched my daughter hug him, I stepped up to hug him, too. I thanked him and told him how blessed we had been to have him and we told him goodbye.

Just like that, he was gone.

When Denise met me to deliver Petro the day we bought him, she said, "Tell Lacy that this is the one man who will never break her heart." She was wrong. Our hearts were so broken.

29

And I heard a crack in my spiritual armor deep within my heart and my soul... at the core of my very being. A deep soul wrenching sound of faith shattering, of trust shaking, of the most indescribable grief, and, yes, anger at a God that I had so loved and trusted.

In the past, I often had times of disappointment, doubt, disillusionment... but never anger.

It wasn't that I never expected anything bad to ever happen. It wasn't that we expected or deserved a blessing such as Petro. It wasn't that I no longer believed in God. I just didn't know why a loving God would bother to give my child such a blessing and then, just as quickly, take it away. It just seemed so cruel.

I saw my daughter, who I had taught everything I knew about our wonderful, beautiful, heavenly Father, and about faith in a kind and loving God who sacrificed His own son for us... withdraw into a dark place where she wanted no part of such a God. For the first time in my life, I had no answers for her. It was a dark place indeed.

It's when a man is cracked that the light is able to get through.
(*Jeffrey Lewis*)

It's hard to describe those days. There was a deep sadness, numbness, and grief. What was most devastating was the absence of my belief, not in the existence of God, not in the assurance of salvation, but in His goodness. Again, I questioned His presence and His plan for my life. I hate unanswered questions and a life that feels out of control. With questions always comes doubt. And with doubt always comes fear.

Satan was whispering, sometimes shouting, in my ear. Does He even bother with someone like you? Does He hear you? Does He care? Or, maybe it was just my own wondering which one of my failures had required the sacrifice of my daughter's joy. There were so many thoughts, doubts, and fears that I had never faced before.

Take me Lord, punish me Lord, test my faith. But what could possibly be the purpose of punishing my child, who was trying hard to believe in you, in the middle of this world full of so much ugliness and pain?

I just did not know how to have a life without faith. God was, and is, my only hope. Without hope, there is no reason to live. Without faith and trust in a loving God, my life has no purpose.

So through my pain and tears, I once again resigned as general manager of the universe, looked up from the deep well of spiritual darkness, and remembered the message displayed by Glenda and Kenny McMullen at the moment of greater loss than ours.

No matter what tomorrow brings... I will praise the Lord.

That very same week, I heard a new song by Casting Crowns called

Praise You In This Storm, and I thought of the circumstances in which it was written. It was a father's cry for healing for a child with cancer.

The answer that he wanted (healing of an earthly body) never came.

The words to that song brought back the lesson I had learned from the McMullen family.

Our loss was a horse and a chance for earthly fame and glory, but my child was still with me.

So far in my life, God had taught me about true faith through a woman of true faith. He had spared my life through a horse accident. And, now, He had spared my daughter's life.

Sometimes the storm itself keeps us from seeing the true blessing.

Now it was my job to help my daughter find her way, through this storm, in a life that is one storm after another.

If we claim to love and serve God, we can't just love and serve Him when things turn out the way we want. That is not love. Love is what God did for us by sending His son to die for us. If that were all He ever did for us, it would be enough. That is the nature of God: pure, sacrificial, perfect love.

Some things will happen as a result of sin that runs rampant in a fallen world. None of them change the nature of God.

Petro died by trying so hard to keep himself from falling head first. He broke his leg and ultimately died. But, my daughter was safe... and lived. How many times in life does it look as if God was absent in the midst of a storm, but His presence was the only reason we came out on the other side?

We are so often unaware of the times when our prayers are answered in a way that we can never (in this life) understand.

I told my heart broken daughter, "We are not going down defeated. We need to find another horse."

> God will help you deal with whatever hard things come when
> the time comes. *(Matthew 6:34)*

> Greater is He that is in me than he that is in the world. *(1 John 4:4)*

I was counting on it.

Unenthusiastically, Lacy agreed to try to find a horse to retain her college scholarship.

Once again, the search was on.

I'd love to tell you that it was so easy, and everything just fell into place. That it was a dream come true. It wasn't. It was a nightmare.

I called every good barrel horse trainer I knew. I answered every promising "for sale" advertisement I saw. We drove thousands of miles and tried countless horses. Nothing was even close. A few kind people, trying hard to help, allowed us to take their horse and try them. Some of these were proven winners.

Unbelievable things were happening (as if things could get worse). Horses that had never run off... ran off. Horses that had never ducked before (turned before a barrel)... ducked. Lacy tried four different horses at four college rodeos and got four "no-times."

She said, "No more... I'm done." And she meant it.

But God wasn't done, and neither was I.

Then one day, I got a phone call from Denise. The beautiful woman of God who had endured some storms of her own and sold us her most prized possession, Petro.

Of course, she too was heartbroken when he died. This is what she said, "I do not feel like this is the end of Lacy's story, and I feel like God has put it on my heart to help her find another horse. I have been praying about it, and I think I know where he is. He is a paint horse and his name is Petey.

As Denise began to tell me about this horse, I said, "Oh I know Petey. I heard they might sell him and had made arrangements to try him. But at the last minute they changed their mind about selling him."

The young lady who owned him said that Petey had been the one thing that had healed her heart when she had lost the best horse she ever had (sound familiar?) and she just couldn't sell him. That had been several months before. However, Denise said something had happened within the family, and they now needed to sell him. Today. She said if I wanted him, I had better call today. I hoped I was hearing God right.

I called, made an offer, and bought him over the phone... not something a person in their right mind would do. Well, at this point, nobody would say that I was in my right mind. I just felt God at work once again.

So I met them at a barrel race to pick up MY new paint horse. I never really liked paint horses. I remembered that saying about the reason Indians rode paints. Apparently, they were the only ones they could catch on foot!

As she unloaded him, I noticed a lot of scratches down the side of her trailer and some wires hanging down where lights used to be. "Oh yea," she said, "Petey did that.... he doesn't like to be alone." Oh my.

She handed me the lead rope and added, "I hope Lacy has a lot of patience, she's gonna need it!"

So began our journey with the strangest, most aggravating, almost human, most amazing horse I have ever seen.

There is nothing so good for the inside of a man as the outside of a horse.
(Mark Twain)

There was just one small detail to work out. My daughter had QUIT barrel racing. I called to tell her about Petey, and she said, "That's great Mom... you ride him... I'm done. If God had wanted me to run barrels, He wouldn't have taken my horse." This could be a problem.

So I was riding MY new barrel horse one day, which was quite the experience because Petey only had one speed... wide open. Lacy was watching, from a distance, in the roping pen. So I gave up trying to lope a circle, thought I might as well give it a shot, and headed toward the first barrel...at that one (wide open) speed. And, it was outstanding! This horse may not be playing with a full deck, but he could run a beautiful set of barrels.

And, after seeing her overweight, middle aged Mom make a pretty amazing run on the big paint horse... the girl who swore she would never run barrels again decided to give it one more shot.

I could give you a list of Petey's accomplishments, and they were plenty, but that was only a small part of the role Petey played in our lives. For the first time in a really long time, we laughed.

Petey was a very intelligent, entertaining clown. Lacy spent most of her time holding him because if you left him at the trailer alone, he would most likely tear something up. If you left the saddle compartment open, he would unload it and stand on all your tack.

He was also very dramatic. If he had a slight stomach ache, which he often did, he would run to you and put his head against your chest. If he could have sat in your lap with his head on your shoulder, he would have.

He could take off any winter blanket you put on him. I looked out one morning when it was snowing, and he was running with his blanket in his teeth and waving it as if to say, "Hey mom... I'm gonna need this back on!"

It was hard to take life too seriously when Petey was around. Plus, he was good at his job. He was the most consistent, honest, barrel horse I had ever seen. He didn't win a lot of firsts, but he placed about 70% of the time in all levels of competition. I could show you videos of 100 runs, and they would all look exactly alike.

He was even better at his other job... healing Lacy's broken heart.

In Lacy's last year at TSU, at the last college rodeo, I sat in the same building where it began with Petro, and watched her become the Southwest Region NIRA barrel racing champion. This time I cried different tears. It wasn't gratitude for winning, even though I was very grateful. It was gratitude for restoration of faith and healing of a young girl's heart.

Sometimes God so obviously does things and blesses you in a way that leaves no doubt as to where the blessing came from... just because He loves you and He wants you to know that. And, just because He can.

Much like people, Petey was given a talent, not for his glory, but for God's glory through him. He had a very special spirit, and he was placed in the hands of more than one person that needed spiritual healing.

Championships are nice, but they are really pretty insignificant in the big scheme of things. But when God does something in a way that you have no doubt that the gift was from Him, that is life changing. When you just feel him saying, "I care about your tears and your pain, and I know you can't understand, but I want you to be assured that I am always with you… and I love you." Nothing this world has to offer can compare.

> All things work for good for those that love God and are
> called according to His purpose.
> *(Romans 8:28)*

People say, "Everything happens for a reason." I don't really believe that. I believe we live in a broken, fallen world where evil is alive and well. I do believe that everything is under the control and sovereignty of God, and anything that happens has to pass through Him.

But in this world, He also allows free will and consequences, which began when Satan chose to try to take God's place, and the battle for glory began on earth.

I believe God allows us to see both good and evil so that we get a taste of both heaven and hell on earth. Then ultimately and eternally, we get to choose.

I don't know exactly why Petro came to us, and then was taken away just as quickly. Some things we will never understand. I don't have to. I just choose to trust the One who does.

I want to be the person who praises God in the storm. Not only when He gives us the things we want in the way we want them, but even when He takes them away to bring us to Him. And, in the middle of the storm, if God shows up, it was worth every tear.

I'll praise the God who allows…and restores.
I'll praise the God who gives… and takes away.
I'll know that in, and through, all things…He is good.

7

𝓐ngel in 𝓑lack

Angels are watching. They mark your path.
They superintend the events of your life and protect
the interest of the Lord God, always working to promote
His plans and to bring about His highest will for you.
(Billy Graham)

Song: Angels Among Us *(Alabama)*

He has put His angels in charge of you
to watch over you wherever you go. *(Romans 8:18)*

I'm pretty sure I saw my first angel in the middle of Highway 281 on November 17, 2003. He was dressed like Johnny Cash... all in black.

There was good reason for that. Black is easiest to see in the fog.

It was a typical Sunday morning for us in those days. We left at 7:30 a.m. and headed to a high school rodeo, with two kids asleep in the back and four horses in the trailer.

What was not typical, however, was the fog. It was so thick that visibility was probably not much more than 30 feet.

I had been doing music at our rodeo's church service for several years. Since they felt the need to have the rodeos on Sunday due to so many kids being involved in other sports, we would just have a short church service between events. On this particular Sunday, I was going to give my testimony.

I had chosen a song called *How Could I Ask For More (by Cindy Morgan)* to sing as a part of that testimony. This is a song about learning what is really important in life and being grateful for it. I had changed a few words to fit my own life.

At the conclusion of that day, I could add a whole new verse.

I put the tape in the CD/tape player and began to practice the song. THANK YOU LORD, HOW COULD I ASK FOR MORE?

This is a song about being grateful for the simple things that we so often take for granted... being able to kiss your mama goodnight or hold on to daddy's hand. Things like dancing in the dark with someone you love or just holding a sleeping baby in your arms. Amazingly beautiful things that bless our lives in so many ways.

I had learned some hard lessons in life, very young, and I was truly grateful for small blessings.

I had also learned how quickly things can happen and how quickly life can change. And I was about to learn one more.

I distinctly remember at the moment I sang the words, "Thank you Lord, how could I ask for more?", I looked up and there was a semi-truck pulling across the road. I thought I calmly said (my kids said I screamed), "Do you see that truck?" And we slammed into him at probably 60 miles an hour.

The thing I relived the most, for months, when I closed my eyes, was the sound of the impact. It was deafening. Then, there was silence. It was like all my senses shut down. Glass was flying by in slow motion. I remember the feeling of spinning and not being able to control my body. When we came to a stop, it was so quiet... except for the birds... I could hear birds singing.

The left side of the truck was gone... doors, windows, tires, everything. The back had been smashed into the front of the cab by the trailer. I turned around to look at my children and they were gone. Time stood still. I will never forget that feeling.

As I went around to the left side, I could see that both children were lying in the floorboard partially under the front seats. Both were unconscious. The truck had spun around in a direction that kept everyone in the truck. That may have been miracle number one.

I was the only one wearing my seatbelt. We were only a couple of miles from home, and Mom had not turned to say, as she had a thousand times before, "Put your seatbelt on."

36

Earlier that year, I had some major surgery for some tumors (which turned out to be benign), and I had done some major studying in God's word about healing and claiming God's promises. This is an area I have always struggled with. I always felt that claiming healing, with a faith that did not doubt, was hard. God could always say no. It felt like I was bossing God around.

Apparently, I had absorbed those verses I had been memorizing because a friend who lived a mile away said I was screaming them at the top of my lungs. I do remember praying and speaking Psalm 91, "He will send His angels to watch over you..." And I shouted, "You promised God... now you send them!" And then from 2 Kings, "I have seen your tears, and I have heard your prayers, and I will heal you."

I'm not proud that I was ordering God around, but I was a scared mother, in shock, and desperate for God to help us.

By this time, Jay (my son) sat up and kept asking, "What's wrong with Lacy?" I quickly explain, and then he says, "OK, I'm going home now" and would try to get out of the truck. He repeated this scenario about every 10 seconds. Concussion.

Lacy is still unconscious, and I am still crying and praying over her as I have been for some time. Her Dad, who has no front teeth and has bitten thru his tongue, is apparently tired of hearing her mother being hysterical, so he comes over and says so matter of factly, "Lacy wake up!" And she wakes up. Now why didn't I think of that?

At the same time, I heard screaming from the side of the road. "Get away from the truck!" Only then did I realize that we had come to a stop across the middle of the highway, still in thick fog. There was another semi-truck coming at full speed.

Suddenly, there was a man dressed in a black shirt and black pants in the middle of the road waving his arms to stop the truck. He never waivered. With brakes squealing, the truck was barely able to stop before hitting him. It appeared to have stopped up against his chest. Then he was gone.

I'm not sure how many miracles happened that day. Our injuries were minor in comparison to the extent of the impact and the damage to the truck and trailer. Two of the horses died, and one was never able to run again. Lacy and Jay's grandparents, who were on their way to the hospital, not knowing the extent of the injuries, passed the wrecker with the truck and trailer. They said they discussed the fact that those could not be ours because no one could have survived that.

We did.

Even though I am a huge believer in seat belts, and I am ashamed that we even started the truck without the kids having theirs on, it may have been a blessing. In this instance, on the side that my husband and daughter were on, the top of the seat was severed, and, had they been strapped in, that would have been where their heads were. Ironically, had I not had mine on, I would have gone through the windshield. These things were exactly what had to happen to save us.

I believe it is possible that God healed my children on the spot. It is possible. I also believe He protected us from death... not from catastrophe, or pain, or loss. Those are inevitable things of this world. It was not our appointed time to die. Or maybe because of a mother's desperate plea, God gave us more time, just as He did in 2 Kings 20 with King Hezekiah. I believe there are miracles that happen every day that we may be unaware of.

I do know this: There was an angel that protected us that day. He was visible because he needed to be. I was the only one who saw him. I believe that was God's gift to me; that I would see... and know.

Whether it was a human angel or one of God's supernatural angels, doesn't really matter. He saved us. And, as He promised, God was with us.

When I get to heaven, and I finally get to meet my angel, and I finally get to thank him personally... I will know him immediately. He'll be the one dressed in black.

> Now you've seen and you believe but blessed are those
> that never get to see and they believe anyway. *(John 20:29)*

I believe.

8

Happily Ever After

Happily ever after is just how it oughta' be
Love that's given away is never free
Life in desperation finds a truth it can believe
My heart just found no peace in reality
So make believe was good enough for me
(song I wrote: Waitin' On A Fairy Tale)

Keep me from lying to myself... turn my eyes
from worthless things and give me life through your word.
(Psalm 119:29 and 37)

Divorce is one of the most devastating defining moments that any human can go through. I wouldn't wish it my worst enemy.

After I was through wondering how a fairly intelligent human being could be so stupid, I had to take a pretty hard, honest, look at myself. It comes with the territory.

Every little girl dreams of the fairy tale marriage. Well, in my day, we still dreamed. It seems that young people today are exposed to so much more through movies, television, and social media, that the dream isn't as anticipated as it once was. Today, it's more like, "Well maybe we'll give it a shot, and if it doesn't work out, we'll just move on." Moving on looked like failure to me, and I was never good at accepting failure.

I am also a positive thinker, and my natural instinct is to believe the best in people. I am also a little stubborn when I set my mind on something. I needed a knight in shining armor to come and take me away, and I was determined to have him. I needed a fairy tale.

I believed I would create the perfect family that I never had. So I chose the guy that fulfilled all the requirements. I saw him as the all-American young man. He didn't drink, smoke, or cuss. He had a wonderful Christian family. His parents had been happily married for many years (now over 50). He attended church on Sunday. He was very driven about accomplishing his goals in the rodeo world. He was nice looking, funny, and convinced me that he loved me. This was it. Happily ever after. Absolutely.

After a lot of years of studying psychology, and a few years of counseling for myself, I've discovered a lot about human beings... such as myself.

We are all born with a large empty hole deep inside. We try our whole lives to fill that emptiness. For some, it is the quick fixes: drugs, alcohol, sex, food. Or it may be a job, money, success, awards, and achievement. But at one time or another, almost all of us believe it will come from another person. A spouse, or someone we love. Maybe even our children. THEN... we will be happy and live happily ever after.

And, some of us are so hard headed that anything less than that looks like failure and is unacceptable. So, if reality is unacceptable, we create a fairy tale reality that we can live with.

I'm not sure when I developed my ability to block out reality and create my own perception of my world, myself, and the world around me. Somewhere along the way however, I became very good at it.

And I (unknowingly) filled that emptiness with a lie.

There is a difference in the "learning to be content" that Paul talked about in Philippians 4:11 and living in denial. Denial served a purpose in my life that enabled me to be happy and content with my life (even when I had every reason not to be)... for awhile. I had not learned to be content with the truth. I would not face the truth. I was content with the truth I created... which was a lie.

The problem is, real life often becomes so overwhelming that your own heart can no longer believe the lie. It's like sitting in the theater when the movie is over and sitting in silence as the credits (in your case the list of facts of your life) roll across the screen, and you are stunned by the moral of the story. What ever happened to "Happily Ever After?"

My uncle Peter, who was my most eccentric relative, spent years studying palm reading. My mother, who was his sister, spent many years studying handwriting analysis. We had some very interesting family gatherings which always involved the "revealing" of personality traits of the family members. I can remember as a teenager, Uncle Peter looked at my palm and said it was like I had no life before I was 12 years old. Not sure how that works, but apparently it was not evident in my hand. I'm not sure where the gift of palm reading comes from, but I do know he had a gift. Actually, he stopped a few years later when he was convicted by what he read in scripture and a feeling that it was probably not a gift from God.

I often wondered, if there was any truth to it, if maybe the reason he saw nothing was because all I could remember of my childhood was the pain, so I blocked it out. I couldn't remember the good parts of my childhood without remembering the bad. So I just didn't think about it at all.

I was determined to never have to feel those feelings again. These are the things I would have bet my life I would never let happen in my family. And I would have given my life to spare my children from the same pain that I had endured.

I can see now that I sacrificed my self-respect, my dignity, and my value as a human being to avoid that reality.

I married a man who was away from home six months out of the year. That allowed me plenty of time to create my own fairy tale marriage. My brother said, "You have the perfect marriage… you never see each other!"

When he was home, he was more than happy to play out the fairy tale. But reality was only the next trip away.

I think that is my explanation to "How could you be so stupid?"

Because I am such an analytical person, I have spent many years trying to figure out what happened. I believe that we were kids who loved each other, in our own broken way, and started with good intentions. Unfortunately, we are all broken human beings who look to someone else to make us whole.

I believe my husband tried to fill the empty hole in him with winning and the applause and approval of the world. At some point, when life wasn't fulfilling that for him, he stepped into another of those quick fixes that became an addiction. And that addiction became a lifestyle.

And Satan smiled.

I believe I tried to fill that emptiness with a vision of a perfect husband and family. And when that was slipping away, I turned toward my children and my role as a mother. It was safer to love them.

The only difference between us was, when all else failed, I ran to God. My husband ran the other way…to other women.

As much as I wanted to have a marriage that allowed us to live happily ever after, some things just can't be fixed. Don't get me wrong, I know God can fix anything, but you have to give Him all the pieces, and let go of the things of this world that we hold on to.

You can make your own choices, but you can't choose your
your own consequences.
(Joe H. Williamson: Cowboy preacher)

God never said He would take away all the consequences of our choices. He said there was forgiveness and unconditional love if we put our hope and trust in Him. But often, the consequences last a lifetime.

God did not call sin a sin and tell us to stay away from it to take all the fun out of life. He told us to stay away from it because it destroys us... one tiny little wrong choice at a time.

There is only one thing that will fill up that emptiness inside every human being: A relationship with our heavenly Father. It is how we were created. I believe if God, and His word, had been what we based our life and our marriage on in the beginning, we would be still working on that happily ever after.

I have definitely learned that there is only one perfect love, one perfect Father, one perfect plan. All the rest of us are imperfect and broken. That is reality.

And I know there's only one... One and only perfect love
From a God whose word is not a fairy tale
And when they lay me down to rest... My final chapter is the best
I know exactly how my story ends....
"And she lived Happily Ever After"
Forever and ever... Amen

My advice for marriage... from the other side.

Love God first.
Look for someone who loves God first.
Love each other in the same way God loves you.
Love yourself in the same way God loves you.
Communicate...use your words.
Forgive freely.
Be honest.
Set boundaries and stick to them.
Pray together.
Face the truth no matter how much it hurts.
Pick your battles: The ones with eternal consequences most important

It's not about you.

WAITIN' ON A FAIRY TALE
(SONG I WROTE IN 2012
TO THE TUNE OF ME AND BOBBY MCGEE)

Once upon a time was such a long, long time ago
When knights in shining armor filled my dreams
If I could just be perfect, then he'd be perfect too
And he'd take me to a place of love for keeps.

So I gave my heart away and trusted in undying love
And slipped into a dream that could not fail
In my secret place I refused to see what was staring back at me
Truth just has no place in a fairy tale
That's why romance books are easier to sell.

(Chorus)
Happily ever after is just how it oughta be
Love that's given away is never free
Life in desperation finds a truth it can believe
My heart just found no peace in reality
So make believe was good enough for me.

Well I finally woke up from the dream and just had to let it go
And make my "knightmare in shining armor" ride away

44

The moral of the story is sometimes really hard to find
But the one that seems to work is "love is blind."

And I know there is only one, one and only perfect love
From a God whose word is not a fairy tale
And when they lay me down to rest, my final chapter is the best
I know how my love story ends.

(Spoken)
And she lived happily ever after.

(Sing)
Forever   and   ever,   Amen.

9

A Mother's Broken Love

(NOTES FROM MY JOURNAL 2010)

We all come from a broken family, because all
families are broken. Even God's. In our brokenness we
are just where we need to be. Fractured. Messed up. Sinful.
Needy. Redeemable. There is beauty in the broken.
(Elisa Morgan)

Song: Hold on Tighter *(Chonda Pierce)*

The wisest of woman builds her house, but folly with her
Own hands tears it down. *(Proverbs 14:1)*

Last night I opened my window, on a sultry spring evening, and heard
the sound of children. The sound of laughter and the exuberance of youth
played a song in my heart that has been silent for so long. I can't help but
smile in remembrance as longing for the past overwhelms me.

The quiet in my house is deafening. It has been like a ringing in my ears that slowly developed over the years. The silence has become a part of my existence, unnoticed, until the sound of children's laughter reminds me how loud the silence has become.

How did the years get by so fast?

How did a life that was so full become so empty?

Today is Mother's Day. Being a mother is the greatest privilege and blessing that God has ever given me. Even though I have many regrets for things I wish I had done better, I cherish every single day that I have been given as a mother. On this day, in this year, I so deeply regret the dissolution of the family that we brought my children into.

I'm taken back to the feelings I had as a young girl when the security of my family disintegrated. I grieve so deeply for the pain I would have given my life to save my children from. I wonder what small decision, what tiny choice all those years ago started the chain of consequences that ended here with the end of a family, the end of a purpose, the end of life as I have known it for the past 30 years.

Who am I now? I am nobody's wife, nobody's little girl, and a mother to children (young adults) that are struggling to function on their own outside of a family that no longer exists.

For the first time in many years, I think of my own mother's thoughts on her Mother's Day when she was 51, the age that I am today... the age that she died. I believe my mother willed herself to die in the dark hole of depression. Even though cancer took her life, a broken heart took her will to live. After the failure of her second marriage and a husband who threw her away when he moved on to another woman, she could no longer find a reason to go on. She was in the darkest place imaginable: The place of no hope. It is a place of loneliness, despair, sorrow, and regret. She saw an empty life with no one to love or maybe just no one to love her back. Only now can I truly understand that dark place.

I spent many years being angry because she left me... left me at 11 years old when she and my dad had nothing more to hang on to. Leaving me at 23 when I had so many more years to need a mother's guidance and love. I only knew that I needed her, and she was gone. In my selfishness of youth, I did nothing to ease her pain or lift her from that dark place.

I understand the great sadness and the dark place. But I hope I never lose sight of what gives me real hope. I have hope for a new purpose that God has for me in the next chapter of my life here on earth. I have no desire to leave my children to this difficult life even one minute before I have to. On the empty days and the long quiet nights, I feel the love of a heavenly Father that has had a hand on my shoulder, and His arms around me, for as long as I have memory of life.

I have a daughter that is so much more of a gift to me than I was to my own mother. She is a loving young girl, with an old soul, that feels deeply and compassionately for the pain of others. She has been a very undeserved gift to me since the day she was born. I pray for the day when her faith overcomes her anxiety and fear and her spirit finds the peace that passes all understanding. In spite of her battle with fear, she is my rock, and in my later years, she is my best friend.

I have a son who is so much like his mother in ways that he would never admit. He feels deeply, analyzes incessantly, and has a deep sense of right and wrong. He makes me laugh and makes me cry sometimes all in the same day. But, he is much more comfortable pushing things away that hurt too much to feel. It is that place far enough away from the heart that you can still breathe. I know that place well.

I grieve for the pain I have added to their lives. I pray that God will give me the wisdom and the time to help them through this place that I have also been. Elisa Morgan, in *The Beauty of Broken*, writes:

Here's the thing: I thought it was my fault that my first family broke, so I
was determined it was my responsibility to make an unbroken family in
my second one. Problem is, I'm broken. Everybody is. So no matter what
we do, we all end up making broken families. In one way or another.

On this Mother's Day, I wish I could tell my mom that I am sorry and that I forgive her. I wish I would have been there for her. But I know that she is in a place where she can finally feel the unconditional love that she could never find here on earth.

I am so thankful for children that have given me a glimpse of what real love is. The way a mother loves her children is the closest we will ever come to knowing how much God loves us.

Today, regret will visit, but it will not live in my heart. It will not find a home there. The beauty is in the lessons that we have learned. I am broken but the brokenness will not rule my life.

We all come from a broken family, because all families are broken.
Even God's. In our brokenness, we are just where we need to be.
Fractured. Messed up. Sinful. Needy. Redeemable.
There is beauty in the broken.
(Elisa Morgan)

It is quiet outside my window now. The laughter is gone. My heart is at peace, and the full moon and the stars remind me how awesome and beautiful God's creation is. Living on this earth is worth it. It is a gift in spite of the pain of human failure. God loved me so much that He let His only son die to save someone broken like me. That is a love that no one can take away.

Mom,

I owe you a debt I could never repay. You gave me life, and you taught me about the God who would be my source of life on this earth, and my only hope for life after this one that will never end. It is the greatest gift you could have ever given me. I never got a chance to thank you for your teaching me about God's love. I'm sorry you lost sight of that love. But I will see you again. I will see that beautiful smile, and hear that infectious laugh, in a place where love never ends.

Happy Mother's Day.

MY MOTHER'S LAUGH
(SONG WRITTEN FOR MY MOM IN 1984)

There are things you take from the ones you love
That you carry inside forever
Very special things…that you can't touch or see
They have the power to hold you tight or set you free
And of these there are so many special things
That are given you by a Mother
Not the least of which is life itself
And if you're lucky… a sister and brother
But of all the things that my Mother gave to me
That will bless my life into the hereafter
I'd have to say one thing I'm most thankful for
Was the sound of her laughter

CHORUS:
Because each time I heard my Mother laugh
I could believe beyond believin'
That no matter how hard this life will seem
It's all just a part of livin'
And now there are days when I look at my life
And wonder how will I ever take it
But when a memory of her laughter comes thru
I know I'm gonna make it

How she made that very special sound
Is still beyond all explanation
But those of us who knew her truly believe

It was one of God's special creations
And even when the world around condemned
She could laugh and still glow like the brightest gem
And even now....only the sound is gone
The spirit of her laughter lives with me from now on.

And when my time on earth is done and St. Peter lets me in
I will know when I have made it home
When I hear her laughter again.

In the sweet by and by
We will meet on that beautiful shore
In the sweet by and by...

I will hear her laughter... again.

In memory of
Greta Joyce Brock
1932-1983

10

My Guardian Angel is Exhausted

I beg you to see that your enemy has a tremendous
investment not only in digging and camouflaging a
pit in your pathway but also, should you tumble down,
in convincing you to stay there after you fall in.
(Beth Moore)

Song: Remind Me Dear Lord
(Jimmy Swaggart)

You have decided the length of our lives. You know
how many months we will live and we are not given
a minute longer. *(Job 14:15)*

I'm not sure why my defining moments of faith seem to frequently
involve a blow to the face. I have come to realize, however, that real
change, and re-focus on what is important, usually involves a blow or a

storm.

It would be nice if God could teach us by allowing our lives to go smoothly, comfortably, and easily. And then we would be so grateful that we never lost sight of Him or our purpose ever again.

Unfortunately, we are human beings, and we need constant reminding. Some of us are more hard headed than others.

On November 4, 2012, I was sprinting my favorite little 4 year old gelding, affectionately named Noah (a man with a willing heart), across the neighbor's coastal field. Here, I feel the need to quote the wife of that great theologian, Bill Engvall (comedian), after he had attempted to become a bronc rider. "The next time you get another STUPID idea like that... COWBOY."

Yes, that was not the brightest idea I have ever had. You see, holes are not always visible in a beautiful field of green coastal grass. I can, however, tell you a sure way to find one. If you run a horse really fast, and he steps in a large hole, if you live, you will now know where that large hole is.

The wise are cautious and avoid danger, fools plunge ahead
with reckless confidence. (Proverbs 14:16)

The next thing I remember was sitting at an intersection, in my truck, thinking I needed to go to one of my children's houses, and not being able to remember where they live. I pulled into the nearest convenience store, got out, and stood in front of the pay phone trying to remember how one of those work.

Normally, when I am riding a horse alone, I keep my cell phone in my pocket. This time, of course, I did not. After a few minutes of standing in front of that pay phone, I gave up and went inside and took a Gatorade out of the cooler and went back out to sit on the curb. I walked right past the store clerk, and he never said a word about the Gatorade I just stole!

I guess my brain was starting to clear at this point, and I remembered about cell phones! Not knowing where mine was, which my children would say is a common occurrence on a daily basis, I went in and asked the clerk if I could use his. Now, here is another problem. I don't remember anyone's phone number. That also is a common daily occurrence, even without a concussion, because in today's cell phones I push a name and not a number! Finally, I remembered my ex-husband's number because he has had the same number for 15 years. I called and told him, "I think I fell, but I can't find my horse!"

Well, he called my son, and he found me sitting on the curb drinking my Gatorade, and I talked him into taking me to find my horse. We found the neighbors trying to un-saddle him after he had been wandering around in the front yard.

My neighbor had been at his barn and had seen us fall. He said he went in his house and told his wife to call 911. By the time he got in his truck and got to the field I was in, I had gotten up and was walking toward him. Noah had also run to him when he saw him. He asked me if I was alright and I answered, "Yes," and I took my horse and walked him home, turned him loose in the yard, got in my truck, and drove away. I've always heard that God especially watches over idiots and little children. Apparently.

Another trip to the emergency room with a concussion, broken fingers on both hands, a black eye, and large swollen lump on the head. Don't worry, once again, my face broke the fall! I was told by a physician that if you take a blow directly to the face, you are not as likely to break your neck. It doesn't do much for your appearance, but gratefully, I am still walking.

The next day, my daughter and I were walking in that coastal field looking for my sunglasses. I looked over at her and thought about how she could be here placing one of those "remembrance" crosses on the spot that her mother left this earth. To be honest, I had one fleeting moment when I was a little excited about the fact that, in the blink of an eye, I could have met Jesus! No pain, no sorrow, no regret. Just over in an instant and then love, family who have gone before, peace, and eternity. What a day that will be.

But November 4, 2012 was not that day.

I was given a blow and another storm to go through that resulted in a new and refreshed spirit. Not instantly. There is always a time of reflection, wondering, questioning, and even sadness. Above all else, God is obviously not finished with me yet.

We have to keep learning that life is never something to be taken for granted. We get so caught up in our ordinary, mundane, routine lives that we forget that this ordinary life is a gift in itself. We are never promised another day, ordinary or extraordinary.

Jesus gives us new life. It is up to us to make it meaningful.
(Tony Evans)

I really hope that it doesn't take any more blows to the head to help me regain my focus and purpose.

My guardian angel must be exhausted.

11

Harmony

Whether you are blessed with soul mates who settle into
the most comfortable room inside you, or with those who
walk with you just a little while, not one of those people crosses
your path by chance. Each is a messenger, sent by God,
to give you the wisdom, companionship, comfort, or
challenge you need for a particular leg of your spiritual journey.
(Traci Mullins)

Song: Loving God Loving Each Other *(Gaither Vocal Band)*

God who makes everything work together
Will work you into His most excellent harmonies. *(Philippians 4:9)*

You don't need anybody.

That statement is one of the most devastating and untrue statements
anyone has ever made about me. It is amazing, however, how hurtful words
find a place to live in the recesses of our mind that allows them to never
completely go away... especially the ones that contain enough truth to
warrant consideration.

What I am... is someone who has learned how to be alone... because I
have been alone... a lot. I see myself as a survivor.

Survivor: One who has a knack for pulling through adversity.
A person who copes well with difficulties in their life.
(Webster's Dictionary)

Survivor sounds much better than loner.

Learning to survive without other people does not mean that being alone is the life I desire. My deepest longing and greatest need involves relationships. I believe God created us that way.

First and foremost, it is the relationship with Him. Secondly, it is the relationship with each other.

The Lord God said, "It is not good for the man to be alone. I
will make a helper suitable for him."
(Genesis 2:18)

However, I do see that He said "not good for the MAN" to be alone. The good Lord knew that poor guy was going to need some help! And right off the bat, he (Adam) followed her (Eve) into sin… and then told God it was her fault. So it began.

Because of the long stretches of time in my life when I was alone or felt alone, I just became comfortable there. When being alone becomes the safest, most comfortable place to be, it becomes easier to retreat to that place for survival. When relationships become challenging and uncomfortable, retreat is my response.

At times I desperately need someone. At times I don't want them. The risk of being hurt just seems too great. Is it any wonder men are confused by women?! It's because we are confused by ourselves! Come closer… go away… it is exhausting.

If I am being honest, however, I am wired with an "I can do it myself" attitude. I believe God creates us with what we will need to survive. Then, life proves to us that we cannot do it alone.

I remember, at 9 years old, feeling such a desperation to run to the front of the church at the altar call to secure my salvation. I needed to make sure that God was with me. It's like I knew that I was not going to have an easy road, and I was going to desperately need Him. I consider that a huge blessing… because I was right.

I designed you to have no sufficiency on your own. My abundance and
your emptiness are a perfect match.
(Jesus Calling: Sarah Young)

I was not a shy child. That, coupled with my "I can do it" attitude, went perfectly with a Mother who loved to sing, dance, recite poetry, and perform.

Consequently, because I was also willing to sing, dance, recite poetry, and perform, my mom loved to have me do all of the above.

Well, we didn't have movies, video games, and smart phones (that make us feel stupid) in 1965. We had to create our own entertainment.

When I sang with the children's choir at church, my mom would have to tell me to "tone it down a little" so they could hear the other children.

Seriously, I loved being the star attraction. I'm sure a counselor could use several sessions to get to the psychology of my need for approval here.

I also distinctly remember my mom trying to teach me to "hear the harmony." She played the piano "by ear" and, of course, sang all the parts of a song "by ear." She could not understand why I couldn't "hear" the harmony in a song. I just couldn't hear it.

As an adult, I still loved to sing. God continued to put opportunities in my life to sing with the traditional church choirs, praise teams, etc. But I always sang the melody.

I also began a music ministry in the non-traditional cowboy setting of barrel races, ropings, and rodeos. In this setting, I chose the songs I wanted, sang in the style I wanted, and made all my own choices. I sang alone, to suit... you got it... me. No need for harmony.

After a 7 year run of doing music at the Texas high school rodeos (that my kids competed in), I put the sound system away and informed God that I was done with that. I told him that I wasn't that good at it anyway, wasn't sure how much good I had done, and, besides, I'm old.

I'm sure God gets a good laugh at my proclamations at times. I believe He probably said, "Now maybe you can stand still and be quiet long enough for me to teach you about harmony."

God who makes everything work together
will work you into His most excellent harmonies.
(Philippians 4:9)

I had been asked to sing a couple of times at a newly formed cowboy church. Even though I felt like maybe God was somehow telling me to go there, I had once again informed Him that there was no way that this was the church that I could make my place of worship.

There had been an article in the paper about the "rules" of this new "cowboy church movement," and I said, "See God! Look at this... it says... "There will be no praise and worship music". What kind of church is that?! Church can be no longer than 45 minutes! The music is supposed to be a country song you would hear in a bar with the words changed so that the typical bar cowboy (trying to change his life) will feel at home! AND... NO ALTAR CALL!" I was positive that God would never call me to THAT church.

Have you ever tried to run from something God was calling you to?

It is like when Larry The Cable Guy says, "I told my wife I would NEVER go shopping with her, so, as I was waiting outside of the dressing room at Victoria's secret…"

Same principle: Men should not try telling their wives what they WILL NOT do. And you just can't run from what God calls you to and be at peace ever again!

One Sunday, I had been asked to sing there and the new pastor, who was not your typical cowboy church pastor, asked me if I would help him put together a music worship team. Even though I never intended to go to church there, I said "sure." And so began one of the greatest experiences and blessings in my life.

That is the way our Almighty God works. When you make yourself available, even if you think it is some form of sacrifice, if you are obedient to God, YOU are always the one who receives the blessing.

We chose an extremely talented couple named Frank and Patti Moreno to head the worship team. Amazingly, I had heard them sing and play a few months before, and I did something really odd. I leaned over to my daughter and said, "I would love to sing with them just one time!"

Patti Moreno sings amazing melody. Nothing I could ever sing could compare, in any way, to her voice. As God would have it, however, she has a very low, uniquely beautiful voice. It's a voice that makes it much easier to sing the harmony parts. And if I were going to be a part of this team, I would definitely have to sing harmony.

Small problem: I don't hear the harmony, and I don't read music.

> Delight yourself in the Lord, and He will give you the
> desires of your heart. *(Psalm 37:4)*

But, somehow, God gave me an ability to hear the harmony with Patti.

I know it was never perfect, and often, I believe, I may have sung on three other people's line during the course of one song. But most of the time it worked. And I believe God blessed the effort.

I developed a love for singing that I had never known before.

Even more amazing, in the midst of the many years we sang together, God blessed me even more by her friendship and infectious joy. She was the gift I needed most of all. God knew that.

I am amazed at how God formed ears to hear and voices to sing in such a way that is absolutely unexplainable. Harmony. One of the most amazing creations of God.

You can teach it, but you can't really explain it.

If you listen to only the harmony alone, it sounds awful. But when blended with all the other parts, there is nothing more beautiful. In the end, it is a beautiful song.

I discovered something else. My time as a part of the group was a blessing that I never could have imagined. They became my friends and my family at one of the darkest, loneliest, times of my life.

It hasn't always been easy. Often, extremely talented people are also a little difficult. Egos, opinions, and personalities sometimes arise in a demanding way. But that is the way relationships, and human beings, are.

Learning to work through those times, until the harmony is right, allowing God to use the gifts He has given us (in spite of our differences and weaknesses), has been the most incredible experience I could have ever imagined.

I do need someone.

Singing alone and being alone has a purpose and I thank God for the ability to do both. But learning to live in relationship to a loving God, AND the beautiful people He places in our lives, is the gift that is among God's best.

> The more completely you devote yourself to Me, the more
> freely you can love people.
> *(Jesus Calling: by Sarah Young)*

> May God...who gives this patience and encouragement....help you
> live in complete harmony with each other as is fitting for followers of
> Christ Jesus. Then all of you can join together with one voice...giving
> praise and glory to God.
> *(Romans 15:5)*

I am a part of the harmony. It is my part in the song, and it is my part in this life. It is not the only part...but it is uniquely mine.

It is beautiful. The blending of all God's creations to become His masterpiece. Alone they are good, but together they are magnificent.

Just as God intended from the beginning.

12

The Great Sadness

You'll never know what you have in Jesus
until Jesus is all you have.
(Corie Ten Boom)

Song: Worn *(Tenth Ave North)*

Why are you in despair, my soul? Why are you disturbed
within me? Hope in God, because I will praise Him once
again, since His presence saves me and He is my God.
(Psalm 43:5)

Even the greatest faith heroes of the Bible were, at times, depressed. David, Job, Jeremiah, Paul. If you have had times of despair (and I believe we all do), you are in good company.

Mark Lowery says that if David had been able to get Prozac, we wouldn't have many of the books in Psalms!

I love God with all my heart. I am so grateful for what Jesus did for me that I can hardly find the words to express it. I am so excited that I will see my family and friends in heaven and we will live forever. Most days, I feel an unexplainable joy. But there are times when a great sadness overwhelms me.

****

This is an excerpt from my journal in 2014:

Life is just so routine. Wake up at the same time every day. Feed the dogs, make breakfast, feed the horses, iron the scrubs, shower, put on make-up, go to the same job that I have been doing for 33 yrs. I'm tired. I hate Monday and live for Friday. My life is full of silence and loneliness. Each day brings more of the same. This has been the most difficult time of my life. I'm lost. Not spiritually, not physically, but I am lost just the same. I don't know what my future (on earth) holds and the control freak in me would like to know.

As a child of God, striving to make this mess of a life matter, I am ashamed to say how empty my life feels. I want to be the rock, the encourager, the eternal optimist who only focuses on God and the hope of eternity. But the present keeps sucking me into despair and loneliness.

If I am totally honest, I sometimes feel like my life is over and I am just floating in the universe. I'm not angry that my life resembles nothing of what I thought it would be in so many areas, but I am sad. My heart of faith knows that God has a plan for me, but my feelings of doubt tell me I won't make it.

Today I'm just not strong enough. I'm losing the battle in my mind. Okay, I'm a little angry. No, I'm not angry. I hate that emotion. I do wonder at times, why the ones who love God the most seem to suffer the most.

I remember in the book, *The Shack,* the main character talks about being overcome by "the great sadness." That's it. The great sadness. Even that makes my sense of failure stronger. I am a Christian. I should be joyful always. I'm not. I'm sorry, but I'm not.

****

And there you have it. Depression. Actually, it was more of just a bad day. Clinical depression are these feelings that last more than 2 weeks and keep you from functioning in daily life. I have been there also.

****

This is the entry from the next day:

Today I can read what I wrote yesterday and wonder who that person was. The great sadness is gone, as quickly as it came. I never understood people who were depressed or suicidal. I thought suicide and living in despair was just selfish and self-centered. I now know that it is sometimes not something you can just talk yourself out of. It is something that happens in the brain that travels deep into the soul and becomes an illness that puts us into the battle of our lives.

When I lost my family, children left home, and went through a divorce, my journey into true depression began. When I couldn't find the strength to get up in the morning and I could not go a day without crying, I went to my physician and asked for help. She prescribed medication. Actually, I had researched them and asked for the one that the side effect was weight loss! I thought there was nothing that would help depression more than losing a few pounds!

In a way, it felt like failure. Failure as a Christian. It seemed to indicate that I just didn't have enough faith. You can't imagine the lies Satan will tell you in the midst of the battle. The medication was a life line for me. If depression is not chemical, then why does medication change it? I am not a different person when I take it. My beliefs, my convictions, my love for God and desire to serve him doesn't change. The chemicals in my brain change. Depression is an illness.

And I don't believe God holds it against anyone who is ill for seeking the expertise of the brilliant people who study and provide medical treatment.

Is God capable of healing everyone? Absolutely. Does he give us doctors and medicine and knowledge to fight the diseases that sin brought into this world? Absolutely.

Max Lucado writes in his book *You'll Get Through This:*

Don't let the crisis paralyze you. Don't let the sadness overwhelm you.
To do nothing is the wrong thing. To do something is the right thing.
And to believe is the highest thing.

I don't take the medication anymore, but I would not hesitate to do so if I needed to. The great sadness still comes, but it usually leaves quickly. The more I have fought the battle with prayer, reading God's word, music, and many tears, the easier it has become.

The thing I hated most about the medication was, along with losing my feelings of despair, I also lost many other emotions. Much of the pain in life comes from caring too deeply. As the medication numbed the pain, it also numbed other feelings. I didn't care too deeply anymore. Some days, I didn't care at all. It was a lifeline for a time that kept me putting one foot in front of the other. But in some ways, I missed the tears and the extreme joy. Emotions are what make us human.

So, for now, I will fight the battle when it comes, with a clear head and many tears. I will be holding on to Jesus's hand and knowing that this too shall pass.

Just know that when you feel that great sadness, it is a universal human condition.

You are not alone.

13

Time to Wake Up

To know the will of God is the greatest knowledge
To find the will of God is the greatest discovery
To do the will of God is the greatest achievement
(George Truitt)

Song: Get Up In Jesus Name *(Gordan Mote)*

Therefore do not be foolish but understand
the will of the Lord
(Ephesians 5:17)

Monday morning. I just hate Monday morning.

I try to wake up saying, "This is the day the Lord has made. I will rejoice and be glad in it." I might say it, but, most Mondays, I don't feel it.

I have not slept past 5:00 a.m. in 15 years. However, in October of 2014, on a Sunday night, the electricity had gone off due to a storm, and my brain decided this would be the day I sleep in. At precisely 5:30 a.m., I heard a distinct male voice say "It's time to wake up!" It was so clear that I actually jumped up.

I sat on the side of my bed for a minute, and then said out loud, "REALLY God, I have been waiting all my life to hear you tell me what to do, really hear you, and THIS is what you've got? It's time to wake up?"

I actually laughed and stumbled out of bed to start my dreaded Monday, sure it was some strange dream. As the day went on, I kept going back to that voice. It was so clear. It was not a voice that I recognized. That thought bothered me a little because, if God spoke to me, I would hope that I would recognize His voice. But would you recognize a voice that you have never really heard?

Maybe it was my frustrated guardian angel!

I wondered why, if God wanted to speak to me, THAT would be an important thing to tell me. After all, I am a habitually early person who has not been late to work in 30 years. But I just kept hearing that voice saying, "It's time to wake up."

Two days later (yes some of us are slower than others, God knows this), it just really hit me. That would be an absolutely extremely important thing for God to say to me. In so many ways, I had been asleep, just going through the motions, living in the past, drifting, surviving, just letting one day turn into another. I lived a lot of days in regret and longing for what was, or what might have been, or for what may never be, or for what others seem to have... totally wasted days. The thought occurred to me. No one knows how many more days they will have on this earth to use for a purpose or to waste.

I know that when I open my mind and heart to seek God's will for my life, and not my own, He will present it to me.

I can honestly say that I am different in a lot of ways since that morning. I realized that I can make a difference, in some way, each and every day that I live. It doesn't have to be in a mission field in South Africa. It can just be in the corner of this world that I live in.

It's time to:
1. Finish the book
2. Write the song
3. Find a new dream
4. Let go of the past
5. Love the unlovable
6. Care about the lost

I can choose to do something, no matter how small, that makes today a day of purpose... a day that makes a difference in someone's life. I can pray for the person I dislike the most. I can write a letter telling someone how important they have been to me. I can buy a stranger's lunch. I can just be different. I can let my light shine in a dark world.

One of the most meaningful things anyone ever said to me was when my friend Patti said, "I just want to thank you for being you." It was such an important thing to hear. I think we spend our whole lives trying to measure up and feeling like we are just never quite good enough. That very simple, seemingly unimportant statement is something that will stay with me for a long time. That is all it takes sometimes. Just one simple statement of love and encouragement. It is something we can all do.

Live each day with a purpose. Even Monday. I get it.

It's time to wake up.

14

Finding the Truth

What really matters is not what we think we perceive, or
what others tell us is the truth, but what God says is the
accurate perception and the truth of any situation.
(Charles Stanley)

Song: Revelation (Third Day)

You will seek me and find me... if you seek me with all your heart.
(Jeremiah 29:13)

Childlike faith came easy for me. I accepted the faith of my mother and
grandmother with very little doubt or questioning. God, and the Bible, just
made perfect sense to me. So even when I had years when I was far away
from God, I never stopped believing in Him or in Jesus as my Savior.

It has been a long journey to come to know God as a Father and friend,
but I have never lost my faith. I feel that I have always known the truth.

I realize that it does not come as easily for a lot of people. I also realize
that many people believe in God (or that there is a God) until something

bad happens in their lives. They lose someone they love, or they just feel like God has never answered their prayers, and they just turn away and no longer believe. Oh they may believe He exists but they do not believe in His goodness.

In 2011, I had the opportunity to correspond with a young man who was a professed atheist. I came to know of him from a newspaper article in the local paper. The article told of a group that he was starting at the local University to provide a meeting and fellowship once a week for fellow non-believers.

It made me a little sad but also curious. I wondered what the stories would be that led each of those young people to come to the conclusion that there was no God.

In my mind, just looking at nature and the universe and the human mind and body would be enough to know that there had to be something greater than anything we can conceive. It has to be much more of a challenge to try to think He doesn't exist than to believe in God and His word.

So, I wrote to this young man. Enquiring minds want to know!

I was especially careful to let him know that I was a Christian, but I did not judge them in any way. I was just interested in how he came to his decision to be an atheist. He was very polite and articulate and was willing to talk to me about his decision.

As with many, he was raised in a Christian home and had lost his faith when tragedy struck. His mother died. God did not answer his prayer. So in his hurt, disappointment, and anger, he decided there was no God. And, he explained, if there was a God who let things like that happen, he wanted no part of Him.

I shared a little about my own beliefs and told him I would be praying for them, which greatly offended him. It is strange that it bothered him that I would pray for him to a God in which he did not believe. I actually believed that somewhere in this young man's heart, he knew there was a God. He was just lost in his feelings of anger and betrayal. It happens a lot in this evil world.

Phil McClendon, former pastor at St. John's UMC in Stamford, Texas stated: "If you love God only for what He can do for you, your praises on Sunday will turn to curses by Friday."

In the end, I just asked him to please do one thing. He had made a decision that was going to influence many young lives. I assured him that he did not have to accept my, or anybody else's, beliefs. But it was eternally significant and extremely important that he have good reason for what he was impressing on others. If nothing else, I would hope that his group was an opportunity to search for the TRUTH... that this is what they would see as most important. Nothing more and nothing less. Just the truth.

Christianity, if false, is of no importance, and if true
is of infinite importance. The thing it cannot be is
moderately important.
(C.S. Lewis)

I wanted him to understand that if he was wrong, the consequences for those he influenced would be eternally devastating.

I gave him the name of some books that were written by atheists who set out to disprove God and the Bible, such as *The Case for Christ* by Lee Strobel. He actually thanked me for my correspondence and said that he would consider checking those out.

I'm not sure what happened with him or his group, but my prayer will always be that they sought and found the truth.

After many years of living with someone who struggled with his beliefs, I discovered one thing. Some people will look for a reason to believe. Some will look for a reason not to.

Those who look for a reason "not to" look at the people in the church and the consequences of evil in the world instead of looking into the face of God and into the heart of His word. Anything less than God himself will always disappoint you.

The truth will come from genuinely asking God to show you. We have to have the help of the Holy Spirit to understand God and His word.

The man without the spirit does not accept the things
that come from the spirit of God, for they are foolishness
to him, and he cannot understand them because they are
spiritually discerned.
(1 Corinthians 2:14)

Everyone needs to find their own truth. You cannot just accept your parent's, or pastor's, or friend's beliefs without searching for your own. If you do, the first time you feel betrayed, hurt, heartbroken, devastated by life or death, your doubts will overwhelm you.

And you will have doubts.

It is through those times when things don't make sense that we come to know God the best... if we run toward Him and not away.

A season of suffering is a small price to pay for a clear view of God.
(Max Lucado)

If you need an example of how God cares enough to give you what you need when you are questioning, and searching, and doubting, take a look at Thomas... the most famous doubter of all. Doubting Thomas.

Thomas had seen Jesus and had witnessed miracles. He was one of the chosen. He believed Jesus was the Son of God. But when Jesus was crucified, Thomas believed his eyes, and his heart did not trust what he could not see.

When the disciples told him that they had seen the Lord, Thomas said:

> I won't believe it until I see the wounds in His hands
> and put my hands in the hollow of his side.
> *(John 20:25)*

Jesus could have just not bothered with someone whose faith had been weak. I'm sure he had more important things to do than to show Himself to someone who had already been shown so much. Instead, because Jesus loved Thomas and knew his heart, He showed him the truth.

> A week later his disciples were in the house again, and Thomas
> was with them. Then he said to Thomas: "Put your finger here,
> see my hands. Reach out your hand and put it into my side. Stop
> doubting and believe."
> *(John 20:26-27)*

Then Jesus made one of the most profound statements (to me) in the Bible.

> Because you have seen me, you believe. Blessed are those
> who never get to see, and they believe anyway.
> *(John 20:29)*

Not much you can say to that. So Thomas said, "My Lord and My God."

If you truly want to find the truth, God will take you there. The journey is not always easy. He may take away your burdens, He may take away your blessings. But in the end, like Job and Thomas, you will come to see God. If you want a reason to believe, you will find your truth.

And if you are looking for a reason NOT to believe, I pray you never find it.

Conclusion

Fourteen Stones...
Stones that remind me...

...of the sound of His voice and the assurance of His presence
...of a longing for home and a promise of heaven
...of the beauty of all God's creatures great and small, good and bad
...of our brokenness that can only be healed by a perfect Father
...of a God whose answer is always the best one
...to be grateful for second chances with no guarantee of a third
...of the truth of God's word as the basis of life.

There will be more rivers to cross, more miracles of a great, loving, and powerful God, to see me to the other side. And I will pick up more stones and lay them on the other side, beside the still waters, to remind me... and those that I love... that God is good.

God will keep writing my story, and I will keep singing His song.

May it be a sweet, sweet sound to your ear.

Blessings to all who see the stones,

Cathy J. Hollabaugh

Made in the USA
Columbia, SC
13 January 2020